AF413308

Dedication

Thank You, Lord God.

This guide is lovingly dedicated to my sister in Christ, Mikey. Through her obedience to the Holy Spirit, this devotional was brought to life. She challenged me to look beyond the surface and deeper into who God has called me to be, and for that, I am forever grateful.

I also want to extend my heartfelt thanks to my husband and children, my parents, and extended family and the entire "A Village of Women" community, my sister Elisha, Mama Rhonda, Tinishia and Raquel. Your unconditional love and unwavering support have carried me through the ups and downs, and I am profoundly blessed to walk this journey out with you all.

Table of Contents

Preface

This practical guide is here to help you check and adjust your posture. Prayerfully, it is encouragement to be intentional. Each day or week, as you sit with these reflections, I challenge you to ask yourself: "How am I postured before God today?" Maybe you need to stand firm in faith, bow in surrender, or sit in peace and just let Him be God. Wherever you are, this is your chance to realign.

How are you showing up before God? Are you approaching Him with trust or hesitation? With openness or fear? Your spiritual posture matters. It shapes how you hear God, respond to His Word, and navigate life's ups and downs.

It's personal, and powerful. Through these pages, I expect you to find strength to face whatever comes your way. Use this devotional in the way that best fits your life. Let it guide your mornings and help you to reset and refocus. If you choose to read it weekly, take time to dig deep into each reflection and carry its truths with you. Show up, reflect, and posture yourself for the goodness God has waiting for you.

With Love and Grace, *Coach V*

Posture of Trust

Proverbs 3:5-6
"Trust in the Lord with all your heart and lean not on your own understanding; in all your ways submit to Him, and He will make your paths straight."

Trust is the foundation of every posture we will take before God. It's in trusting Him that we let go of fear, doubt, and the need for control. Trust means acknowledging that His ways are higher than ours and that His plans are always for our good. Maybe work is draining the life out of you, your business isn't moving like you planned, or family issues have you feeling like you're on your last nerve.

Trust doesn't eliminate challenges but transforms how we face them. When we trust God, we shift from anxiety to peace, from striving to resting in His promises. Trust allows us to release what we cannot handle and place it into the hands of the One who can do all things.

As you lean into this posture of trust, know that God is already at work. He is clearing paths, opening doors, and leading you into His perfect plan. Trust Him fully, even when the way ahead feels uncertain. His faithfulness never fails.

Let's Bring It Home:
What is one area of your life where you've struggled to trust God? Take a moment to write it down, pray over it, and release it to Him. Trust that He is already working in ways you cannot see.

Prayer:
Lord, I choose to trust You with all my heart. Help me to release my need for control and lean into Your wisdom and

understanding. Teach me to walk in faith and surrender, knowing that You are guiding my every step. I am tired of trying to do things on my own. Let my life reflect complete trust in Your plans and Your promises. In Jesus' name, Amen.

Posture of Faith

2 Corinthians 5:7
"For we walk by faith, not by sight."

Today, choose to move forward even when you can't see the whole picture. God is working behind the scenes, even when your situation looks the exact opposite of what you prayed for. I know sometimes walking by faith can feel like walking blindfolded.

Let your faith guide you. Take the next step, no matter how small, and believe God, He will handle the rest. That's where the posture of faith comes in. It's standing up and saying, "God, I don't have all the answers, but I know You do, and that's enough for me."

So, what are you facing today? What feels uncertain or out of reach? Shift your posture. Take your focus off what's in front of you and put your hope in the One who's already in control of the outcome. Faith gives you the strength to keep walking.

Let's Bring It Home:
What's one area of your life where you've been relying too much on what you can see? What step of faith can you take today to trust God's plan, even if it's unclear?

Prayer:
Lord, walking by faith isn't always easy, especially when life feels overwhelming. Help me to shift my focus from what I see to who You are. Teach me to trust You with every step I take, knowing that You are guiding me even when the way feels uncertain. Thank You for being faithful, even when I struggle to be. In Jesus' name, Amen.

Posture of Prayer

Philippians 4:6-7
"Do not be anxious about anything, but in every situation, by prayer and petition, with thanksgiving, present your requests to God. And the peace of God, which transcends all understanding, will guard your hearts and your minds in Christ Jesus."

Regardless if you pray a few words, or long and elaborate, position your heart to connect with God. It doesn't matter if you do so on your knees, sitting in the car, or walking through the chaos of your day. Prayer is where the weight of your worries get exchanged for the peace of His presence. It's where you stop carrying what you were never meant to carry.

Let's be honest, life's obstacles do not make praying easy. Sometimes you're just too stressed. Other times, you're so overwhelmed that you don't know where to start. The good news is, God isn't looking for perfect words. He's looking for a willing heart. A simple "Lord, help me" is enough to shift your posture and open the door for Him to step in.

So, how's your prayer posture right now? Do you feel like you're carrying everything on your own? Or are you laying it all at God's feet? Hand it over. When you do, God promises peace that surpasses all understanding. Whether everything is fixed or not, you can rest on God in prayer.

Let's Bring It Home:
Take a moment to stop and breathe. What's been keeping you up at night? Talk to God about it—no fancy words, just honesty. Then

thank Him for being in control, even when things feel out of
control.

Prayer:
Lord, You know exactly what I'm dealing with right now—the
stress, the struggles, and the things I don't even want to say out
loud. Thank You for inviting me to bring it all to You. Help me to
shift my posture from worry to prayer, trusting that Your peace
will guard my heart and mind. In Jesus' name, Amen.

Posture of Courage

Isaiah 41:10
"So do not fear, for I am with you; do not be dismayed, for I am your God. I will strengthen you and help you; I will uphold you with my righteous right hand."

Step forward in faith despite the fear. I know it gets tough sometimes, and life may throw all kinds of situations at us that make us want to shrink back. Situations that may magnify the voice of fear. You may hear it whispering to you every now and again, and it may be saying "You aren't enough," but fear is a liar and a thief. Make every effort to magnify the voice of God, quiet all the noise for just a second, and look beyond your present circumstances and hear God saying "I am with you."

When you know God is with you, it changes the way you move. You can stand tall in situations that used to make you feel small. You can take risks knowing that, even if you stumble, God is right there to catch you. Courage is a posture—a decision to walk in the strength of God instead of the strength of your circumstances.

So, what are you facing that's testing your courage? Maybe it's a conversation you've been avoiding, a new business move, or simply trusting God in a situation that feels impossible. Whatever it is, shift your posture. Stand firm in the truth that you're not walking through it alone. God is holding you up with His righteous right hand, giving you the strength you need for each step.

Let's Bring It Home:
Where has fear been holding you back? Take a moment to name it. Now, remind yourself of God's promise: He is with you, He will strengthen you, and He will uphold you. Write that truth down and carry it with you today.

Prayer:
Lord, fear has tried to stop me, but today I'm choosing courage.
Thank You for walking with me, strengthening me, and holding me
up when I feel weak. Help me to trust in Your presence and to take
bold steps forward, knowing that You are in control. In Jesus'
name, Amen.

Posture of Love

Romans 8:38-39
"For I am convinced that neither death nor life, neither angels nor demons, neither the present nor the future, nor any powers, neither height nor depth, nor anything else in all creation, will be able to separate us from the love of God that is in Christ Jesus our Lord."

Maybe life has taught you to guard your heart. Maybe people have let you down so many times that it's hard to believe in unconditional love. But God's love isn't like human love. It isn't predicated on how good you've been or how well you're doing in life. It's steady, unshakable, and always available no matter what.

If we could ever truly understand the depth of God's love for us, it would change everything. It would shift our posture instantly. At that moment, I believe many of us would stop living for the approval of others and start living from a place of acceptance by God. But what's stopping us now from realizing that even in our mess, God is right there, loving us fully and completely. It's that kind of love that gives you the strength to love others, even when it's hard.

So, where do you need to embrace God's love today? Is it in forgiving yourself for past mistakes? Is it in showing love to someone who's been hard to love? God's love is limitless, and He's calling you to rest in it, reflect it, and walk confidently in it.

Let's Bring It Home:
Take a moment to reflect on God's love for you. Write down one thing in your life that reminds you of His love; something big or small. Then think about someone in your life who needs to feel that love today. How can you show it to them?

Prayer:
Lord, thank You for Your unshakable love. I don't always feel worthy of it, but I know You love me fully and completely just as I am. Help me to stand in that love and reflect it to those around me, even when it's hard. Thank You for never letting anything separate me from You. In Jesus' name, Amen.

Posture of Rest

Matthew 11:28-30
"Come to me, all you who are weary and burdened, and I will give you rest. Take my yoke upon you and learn from me, for I am gentle and humble in heart, and you will find rest for your souls. For my yoke is easy and my burden is light."

When was the last time you truly rested? Not just slept or sat down for a moment, but actually let go of everything that's weighing you down and let your soul breathe? Rest is not just a physical act but a spiritual posture. It's choosing to pause, trust God with your burdens, and allow Him to renew your strength. In a world that glorifies busyness, rest is an act of faith that says, "God, I trust You enough to pause."

When we rest in God, we find peace that surpasses understanding. We remember that He is in control and that we don't have to strive to earn His love or provision. Rest is a gift that allows us to step back and realign our hearts with His.

As you embrace this posture of rest, let go of the pressures to do it all. Rest is not laziness; it's obedience to a God who calls us to be still and know that He is God.

Let's Bring It Home:
What is one thing you can pause or let go of this week to find rest in God? Commit to creating a moment of stillness where you can reconnect with Him.

Prayer:
Lord, I come to You weary and burdened, seeking rest for my soul. Teach me to lay my worries at Your feet and to trust in Your strength. Help me to embrace stillness and to remember that You

are always in control. Let my rest be an act of worship that glorifies You. In Jesus' name, Amen.

Posture of Strength

2 Corinthians 12:9-10
"But He said to me, 'My grace is sufficient for you, for My power is made perfect in weakness.' Therefore, I will boast all the more gladly about my weaknesses, so that Christ's power may rest on me. That is why, for Christ's sake, I delight in weaknesses, in insults, in hardships, in persecutions, in difficulties. For when I am weak, then I am strong."

Strength is not the act of holding it all together, or the gauge of how well you can fake a smile. Real strength sustains you in any situation and that kind of strength comes from God. At the moments when you feel the weakest, most unqualified, or completely stretched is when God really gets to show His power through you.

Paul's words in 2 Corinthians 12:9-10 hit home because they flip the world's idea of strength on its head. We're taught to hide our weaknesses, but God says to embrace them. Why? Because when you admit your limitations, you make room for His limitless power. Strength isn't found in what you can do, it's found in what God can do through you.

Think about what you're facing right now. Does it feel impossible? Or is it just a struggle to get through another day? Whatever it is, take on the posture of strength. Instead of trying to handle it on your own, admit where you feel weak and invite God's strength into that space. His grace is more than enough to carry you.

Let's Bring It Home:
What's an area in your life where you feel weak right now? Take a moment to thank God for the chance to rely on His strength instead of your own. Write down one way you can lean on Him today instead of trying to figure it all out yourself.

Prayer:

Lord, I'm over trying to be strong on my own. Thank You for reminding me that Your grace is enough, and Your strength shows up in my weakness. Help me to let go of my pride and let You take over. I'm trusting You to carry me through every hardship, knowing that when I'm weak, You are strong. In Jesus' name, Amen.

Posture of Joy

James 1:2-4

"Consider it pure joy, my brothers and sisters, whenever you face trials of many kinds, because you know that the testing of your faith produces perseverance. Let perseverance finish its work so that you may be mature and complete, not lacking anything."

Joy in trials? Really? When life is throwing punches, joy is the last thing on your mind. It's easy to focus on frustration, disappointment, or exhaustion. But James challenges us to see trials through a different lens. He's not saying to put on a facade or to mask your feelings. He's inviting us to consider our trials as opportunities for growth.

Yes it's uncomfortable, but tribulation is a tool God uses to stretch our faith and strengthen our perseverance. The trials that come refine us, making us more mature and complete. Joy doesn't come from the trial itself, it comes from knowing that God is working through it for your good. Trust God even when you can't trace Him. He has a purpose.

It may be tempting, but instead of asking, let joy take root and inspire you to change your posture.

Let's Bring It Home:
Take a moment to think about a trial you're facing. What lesson or strength might God be building in you through it? Write it down, and ask Him to help you see the joy in the growth He's bringing.

Prayer:
Lord, joy is hard to find when life feels heavy, but I'm trusting You to give me a new perspective. Help me to see my trials as opportunities to grow and to lean on You in the process.

Strengthen my faith and fill my heart with joy, knowing that You are working everything out for my good. In Jesus' name, Amen.

Posture of Surrender

Matthew 16:24-25
"Then Jesus said to His disciples, 'Whoever wants to be my disciple must deny themselves and take up their cross and follow me. For whoever wants to save their life will lose it, but whoever loses their life for me will find it.'"

Can I keep it real with you? There was a time in my life when I thought surrendering was a show of defeat. And I absolutely refused to be defeated, no matter what work, family, and all the chaos of life threw my way. I told myself, "I got this," even when it was clear I didn't. And you know what? I was burnt out mentally, physically, and spiritually. I was carrying weights I was never meant to hold.

At some point, I had reached the end of myself, and I broke down and the only thing I could utter in prayer is "God, I can't do this anymore." That prayer wasn't pretty or polished, but it was the truth. I can hardly explain today the release I felt, and the burden that was lifted off of my shoulders at that moment.

That's what surrender looks like, not giving up, but giving over. Letting God carry what you were never built to handle. So, let it all go! The stress at work, your family woes, and all that you believe you need to have figured out? God is inviting you to take on His yoke, a partnership where He does the heavy lifting.

Let's Bring It Home:
What are you holding onto that you need to surrender to God? Write it down and ask Him to help you let it go, trusting that His plan is better than yours.

Prayer:
Lord, I surrender my plans, my fears, and my desires to You. Help

me to trust Your purpose for my life and to follow You with a willing heart. Teach me to find freedom in letting go and joy in obedience. Let my surrender be an act of worship that draws me closer to You. In Jesus' name, Amen.

Posture of Grace

Ephesians 2:8-9

"For it is by grace you have been saved, through faith—and this is not from yourselves, it is the gift of God—not by works, so that no one can boast."

Grace is hard to wrap our minds around sometimes. Especially, in today's time where we are taught to work for everything. The idea of receiving something we didn't earn can at times feel uncomfortable. But that's exactly what grace is, undeserved, unearned, and freely given. It's God stepping in with love and mercy when we've done nothing to deserve it.

I used to believe I had to be perfect for God to love me. I thought I had to check all the boxes, be good, do good, and never mess up to earn His approval. But every time I fell short (and I did, often), I felt like I had failed Him. Ephesians 2:8-9 hits like a ton of bricks. God's grace is not extended to us because we've done for Him, but more so because of what He has already done for us.

Begin praising God in this very moment for His love and grace. It will free you. God isn't keeping score, and He's not waiting for you to earn His favor. Grace is His gift to you, no strings attached.

If you are carrying the weight of guilt or shame, believe His grace has already covered it? Let this be the moment you embrace His grace fully. Just receive it.

Let's Bring It Home:
Take a moment to reflect on this truth: God's grace is a gift you don't have to earn. How does that change the way you see yourself and your relationship with Him? Write it down, and remind yourself of this truth throughout the day.

Prayer:

Lord, thank You for Your amazing grace. I know I don't deserve it, but I am so grateful that you love me anyway. Help me to let go of the need to prove myself and to rest in the truth that I am saved and loved by You, not because of what I do, but because of who You are. In Jesus' name, Amen.

Posture of Forgiveness

Matthew 6:14-15

"For if you forgive other people when they sin against you, your heavenly Father will also forgive you. But if you do not forgive others their sins, your Father will not forgive your sins."

Forgiveness does not excuse what someone did to you. As a matter of opinion offense hurts, it's upsetting and may even linger. Nothing about what's been done to you is okay. However, if you truly want to be free, dare to dive deeper into its power and make an effort to release and let go. Deliberately choose freedom over bitterness. And just so you don't think you're doing anyone a favor; Forgiveness isn't for them, it's for you!

Holding onto unforgiveness is like drinking poison and expecting the other person to suffer. It eats away at your peace, your joy, and even your connection with God. It's a prison where you hold the key but refuse to use it. God calls us to forgive.

It isn't easy. It often feels unfair. But God wants you to trust Him with your pain and to let Him bring healing to your heart. Let it remind us of the grace we've been given. How many times has God forgiven you? When we choose to forgive others, we reflect the heart of God. They're not off the hook with God, but we have to trust Him to handle what we can't.

Let's Bring It Home:
Who do you need to forgive today? It might be someone else, or it might even be yourself. Take a moment to release that burden to God. Ask Him to help you let go and find the peace that only forgiveness can bring.

Prayer:
Lord, forgiveness is hard, but I know You've called me to it. Help me to release the pain and anger I've been holding onto. Remind me of the grace You've shown me, and give me the strength to extend that same grace to others. I trust You to heal my heart and guide me as I take this step toward freedom. In Jesus' name, Amen.

Posture of Purpose

Jeremiah 29:11

"For I know the plans I have for you," declares the Lord, "plans to prosper you and not to harm you, plans to give you hope and a future."

Purpose is one of the greatest gifts from God, it's also one of the hardest things to grasp. We often wrestle with questions like, "Why am I here?" or "What does God want from me?" Life can make us feel like aimless wanderers. Yet, God's purpose for your life is intentional, specific, and filled with hope. And furthermore purpose is not what you do, but it is who you are.

Jeremiah 29:11 reminds us that God's plans for us are good. Even when life feels like it's falling apart, God is still at work, working behind the scenes. Your purpose isn't limited by your circumstances, your past, or even your current struggles. God's purpose is rooted in His promises, not your performance.

Living in your purpose starts with being willing to take the next step. God is guiding you, and while you may think purpose looks like a big, bold move, but more often, it's found in the small, faithful steps you take every day. Loving your family, showing up in confidence at work, or being a light in someone else's life defines your purpose, better than any forged act of labor ever could.

You were created on purpose, for a purpose, and God has equipped you for the journey ahead. The question isn't whether God has a plan, it's whether you're willing to walk in it.

Let's Bring It Home:
Think about the areas in your life where you feel unsure or stuck.

Ask God to reveal how He's working in those spaces and to show you the next step toward living out His purpose for you.

Prayer:
Lord, thank You for reminding me that Your plans for my life are good. Even when I don't understand, I trust that You are working everything for my good and Your glory. Help me to live in the purpose You've created for me, to take each step with faith, and to trust You with my future. In Jesus' name, Amen.

Posture of Faithfulness

Lamentations 3:22-23

"Because of the Lord's great love we are not consumed, for His compassions never fail. They are new every morning; great is Your faithfulness."

Faithfulness is not a simple feat, especially when life is crazy, prayers seem unanswered, or you're caught in a season that feels stagnant. But the beauty of faithfulness lies in remembering who God is. He is steady, and unwavering no matter what. His mercies are fresh every morning, and His love never runs out. That alone is enough to keep us moving forward.

Showing up in prayer, worshipping God through the intervals of life, and standing in obedience is the fuel that keeps you going. Our faithfulness mirrors God's character. Are you faithful in the small things, showing integrity and keeping your word? God sees those moments and honors them. It doesn't have to be a big gesture; Jesus, tells us in Matthew 17:20 to have faith the size of a mustard seed. This kind of faith is found in the small gestures like being consistent, trusting and obeying God daily, and just putting one foot in front of the other, showing up better each day. No matter what season you're in, take heart. God's faithfulness doesn't waver, and neither should yours. This morning is a fresh opportunity to lean on God, trust His promises, and reflect on His continuity in your life.

Let's Bring It Home:
Think about how God has been faithful in your life. Write down one way He's shown His love and compassion recently. Then ask yourself, "How can I reflect that same faithfulness in my walk with Him today?"

Prayer:
Lord, thank You for Your unshakable faithfulness. Even when I doubt, struggle, or fall short, You never fail me. Help me to reflect that same faithfulness in how I live, trusting You in the small and big moments of life. Let my life be a testimony of Your great love and mercy. In Jesus' name, Amen.and Your glory. Help me to live in the purpose You've created for me, to take each step with faith, and to trust You with my future. In Jesus' name, Amen.

Posture of Protection

Proverbs 4:23

"Above all else, guard your heart, for everything you do flows from it."

Your heart is precious, and God calls you to protect it, not just from people who might hurt you, but from the everyday distractions, doubts, and fears that can pull you away from Him. Life has a way of throwing all kinds of things at us, negativity, temptation, stress, and if we're not careful, those things can take root in our hearts. That's why God says to guard your heart "above all else."

Guarding your heart is not a license to shut people out or justification to live in fear. But instead a calling to be intentional about what you allow into your mind and spirit. What are you listening to? Who are you surrounding yourself with? Are you filling your heart with God's truth, or are you letting the world dictate how you think and feel?

Think of your heart as the wellspring of your life. Whatever flows into it will eventually flow out into your relationships, your work, and your daily decisions. When you protect your heart with God's Word and His promises, you're building a strong foundation that nothing can shake.

So, how's your heart today? Are you guarding it, or have you let things creep in that don't belong? God is your ultimate protector, and He's ready to help you fortify your heart with His truth and love.

Let's Bring It Home:

Take a moment to reflect on what's influencing your heart right now. Is it bringing you closer to God or pulling you away? Ask Him to help you guard your heart and keep it focused on Him.

Prayer:
Lord, thank You for reminding me of how important my heart is. Help me to guard it against anything that doesn't align with Your truth. Teach me to fill my heart with Your Word and to trust in Your protection. Let everything that flows from my heart reflect Your love and grace. In Jesus' name, Amen.

Posture of Wisdom

James 1:5

"If any of you lacks wisdom, you should ask God, who gives generously to all without finding fault, and it will be given to you."

Life is full of moments where we just don't know what to do. Decisions about work, family, finances, relationships can leave us feeling stuck or overwhelmed. The world will tell you to rely on your instincts, Google it, or ask a dozen people for advice. But God's Word reminds us of a better option: Ask Him.

God's wisdom is unlike anything we can get from the world. It's not based on trends, opinions, or emotions. It's rooted in truth, purpose, and eternity. God is ready and willing to share His wisdom with you. He doesn't hold back, criticize, or roll His eyes when you come to Him for help. He gives generously, without hesitation.

So, how do you posture yourself for wisdom? It starts with humility. Acknowledge that you don't have all the answers and that you need God's guidance. Then, ask. Not passively, but diligently, with faith that He will answer. Wisdom causes you to trust God to lead you step by step, even when the full picture isn't clear.

His wisdom brings clarity where there's confusion, peace where there's anxiety, and direction where there's doubt. Whatever decision or challenge you're facing, He's ready to guide you. The question is, will you ask and trust Him to show you the way?

Let's Bring It Home:
Think about a decision or challenge you're facing right now. Have you asked God for wisdom about it? Take a moment to pause, pray,

and invite Him into the situation. Trust that His wisdom is available to you, right here and now.

Prayer:
Lord, I need Your wisdom. There are so many decisions I face, and I don't want to rely on my own understanding. Teach me to trust You fully and to seek Your guidance in all things. Thank You for being generous with Your wisdom and for leading me in the right direction. In Jesus' name, Amen.

Posture of Peace

1 Peter 5:7

"Cast all your anxiety on Him because He cares for you."

Peace is something we all crave, but at times can feel impossible to find and like a distant dream to achieve. But God's Word gives us a better way, He asks us to cast our anxieties on Him. Why? Because He cares for us so deeply.

The word "cast" isn't passive, it's active. It means throwing, releasing, and giving up the things that are stealing your peace. God is waiting for you to toss your cares into His hand, like a Father waiting for his son to throw a baseball into his catcher's mitt. And you can bet your bottom dollar that God will not drop the ball! When you release your worries to Him, you make room for His peace to settle in. The kind of peace that is found in knowing that God is in control, even when everything is out of control.

Posturing yourself for peace means choosing trust over fear, faith over anxiety, and surrender over managing every detail of life. It's a decision you make daily, sometimes moment by moment. God wants you to live in His peace and to make it your constant reality.

Let's Bring It Home:
What's been weighing on your heart lately? Take a moment to name those anxieties and imagine handing each one over to God. Trust that He cares for you and is already working it out for your good.

Prayer:
Lord, carrying these burdens on my own is exhausting. Today, I

choose to cast my anxieties on You, trusting that You care for me. Thank You for replacing my fear with Your peace and for reminding me that You are in control. Help me to live in the confidence of Your care. In Jesus' name, Amen.

Posture of Fruitfulness

Galatians 5:22-23

"But the fruit of the Spirit is love, joy, peace, forbearance, kindness, goodness, faithfulness, gentleness, and self-control. Against such things there is no law."

What's growing in your life? How do people know God is working in and through you in theirs? When the Spirit of God is at work in you, His fruit begins to show. Love, joy, peace, patience, kindness, goodness, faithfulness, gentleness, and self-control, these are the marks of a life surrendered to Him. They're not qualities you can fake or force; they grow naturally when you stay connected to the source.

Think of a tree. It doesn't strain or struggle to produce fruit, it just stays rooted. Its job is to remain planted in the right environment, soaking up the sunlight and water it needs to thrive. The same is true for us. When we stay rooted in God through prayer, His Word, and daily dependence on His Spirit, the fruit will come. It may not happen overnight, but over time, His character will start to show in your life. Let God prune what doesn't belong and trust Him to produce what does.

Let's Bring It Home:
What fruit of the Spirit is most evident in your life right now? Which one do you want to see grow even more? Spend time today inviting God to nurture that fruit and to help you reflect His goodness in practical, everyday ways.

Prayer:
Lord, thank You for the gift of Your Spirit and the fruit it brings into my life. Teach me how to stay connected to You so that love, joy, peace, and all the fruits of the Spirit flow naturally through

me. Let my life reflect Your goodness and be a blessing to those around me. In Jesus' name, Amen.

Posture of Renewal

Romans 12:2

"Do not conform to the pattern of this world, but be transformed by the renewing of your mind. Then you will be able to test and approve what God's will is—His good, pleasing and perfect will."

Renewal is a process of transformation that starts in your mind. Allow God to work from the inside out, the outside matters not, if you are broken and jacked up internally. It's like wrapping an empty used box with beautiful gift wrap. But your broken spirit, and contrite heart is what God wants, your transparency, not your well dressed lies. This is actually the peak where some of His best work is done. So be flexible. In Romans 12:2, Paul calls us to resist the pressures and distractions of the world and instead allow our minds to be renewed by God. This renewal shifts our thinking, aligns us with His truth, and equips us to live out His will.

Think about the messages the world sends you daily, how it is always enticing you by trying to convince you, "You need to have more and more" or when you're told to just "Do what feels right." Those patterns can shape your thoughts and actions if you let them. But God's renewal breaks those chains and replaces them with His truth. He reminds you that you are fearfully and wonderfully made, that your worth isn't tied to what you do or possess, and that His plan for you is good.

Renewal isn't a one-time event, it's a daily posture. It's choosing to let God's Word shape your perspective, to filter out what doesn't align with His truth, and to embrace His way of thinking. Over time, this practice transforms how you see yourself, others, and the world around you.

Let's Bring It Home:
What thought patterns or beliefs do you need to surrender to God for renewal? Spend a few moments reflecting on how His Word can reshape your thinking and lead you into transformation.

Prayer:
Lord, thank You for the promise of renewal. Teach me to reject the patterns of the world and to embrace the transformation that comes from Your truth. Renew my mind daily, so I can see clearly and walk confidently in Your will. Let my thoughts reflect Your goodness and purpose. In Jesus' name, Amen.

Posture of Calm

Philippians 4:7

"And the peace of God, which transcends all understanding, will guard your hearts and your minds in Christ Jesus."

Calm is a posture that comes from knowing God's peace is greater than any circumstance you face. You don't have to act like your challenges don't exist or ignore the demands of life. But instead ground yourself in the truth that God is in control and that His peace is available to you in every moment.

The world often equates calm with quiet surroundings or a problem-free life, but the peace of God goes far deeper. It's a calm that shows up in the middle of the storm, not just when the waters are still. This calmness helps us guard our hearts and mind, protecting us from the chaos around us and anchoring us in Christ.

Shift your focus from the noise of life to the presence of God. Whether you're juggling responsibilities, facing uncertainty, or just trying to find balance. God's peace is there to settle your spirit and guide your steps.

Let's Bring It Home:
What's been stealing your calm lately? Take a moment to pause and breathe. Invite God's peace to guard your heart and mind. Remind yourself that His presence is greater than your circumstances.

Prayer:
Lord, thank You for the peace that only You can give. Teach me to posture my heart toward calm, even when life feels overwhelming. Guard my heart and mind with Your peace, and remind me that

You are always in control. Help me to trust You fully and rest in Your presence. In Jesus' name, Amen.

Posture of Obedience

"If you love me, keep my commands."

Obedience is an act of love. Not merely a basis of following a collection of rules. We obey God because we want to honor Him. Remember when Jesus said, "If you love me, keep my commands," He wasn't just throwing His weight around. He is compelling us to show our love for Him through a life that reflects His will.

Living a life of obedience often starts with small, daily decisions. It's listening when God nudges your heart, stepping out in faith when He asks you to, and trusting that His way is better than yours, even when it's hard or doesn't make sense. Obedience always leads to greater peace, purpose, and intimacy with God.

Obedience is meant to be practical. Like speaking kindly to someone when you want to stay silent, forgiving someone who hurt you, or letting go of a plan that you've been holding onto tightly because God has something better. The more you practice obedience, the more it becomes a natural response to His love and guidance.

So, where is God calling you to be obedient today? It could be something big, or it could be a small act of faithfulness. Whatever it is, remember that every step of obedience strengthens your relationship with Him and opens the door to His blessings.

Let's Bring It Home:
Take a moment to reflect on any area of your life where God is asking for obedience. What step can you take today to align your actions with His will? Ask Him for the courage to follow through.

Prayer:
Lord, I want to show my love for You by living in obedience to Your Word. Help me to trust Your plans and to follow Your commands, even when it's difficult. Give me the strength to choose Your way over my own, knowing that You are always leading me toward what is best. In Jesus' name, Amen.

Posture of Patience

"There is a time for everything, and a season for every activity under the heavens."

Ever waited so long for a change in your life that you almost gave up? Maybe you prayed, hoped, and did everything you could, but nothing seemed to move. Then, just when you were about to throw in the towel, something so victorious happened that it left you speechless, proof that God's timing is always perfect. That's patience in action. You're not just waiting aimlessly; you're anchoring your expectation in God who is always working, even when you can't see it.

Patience reminds us that there's a season for everything. Sometimes God is planting seeds in your life that need time to grow. Other times, He's refining you in the waiting, preparing you for something greater than you imagined. The waiting isn't wasted, it's working. God will move in your life; but will you let him be God and rest in His perfect timing.

Think about it: If God gave you everything you wanted exactly when you asked, would you even be ready for it? Patience teaches us to rely on Him, to strengthen our faith, and to recognize His blessings when they come. It's a posture of expectation, not frustration. It's a choice to believe that God is never late, even when it feels like it to us.

What are you waiting for today? Keep trusting, keep praying, and keep expecting. God's timing is always worth the wait.

Let's Bring It Home:
Think about a time when you waited on God and saw His
faithfulness. How does that memory encourage you in what you're
waiting for now? Write it down, and thank Him for what's already
on the way.

Prayer:
Lord, waiting is hard, but I know that your timing is always
perfect. Help me to trust You in the waiting and to see this time as
an opportunity to grow closer to You. Strengthen my faith and fill
me with hope, knowing that You are always working for my good.
Thank You for what You've done and for what You're about to do.
In Jesus' name, Amen.

Posture of Power

Isaiah 40:29-31

"He gives strength to the weary and increases the power of the weak. Even youths grow tired and weary, and young men stumble and fall; but those who hope in the Lord will renew their strength. They will soar on wings like eagles; they will run and not grow weary, they will walk and not be faint."

Have you ever felt like you were running on empty? Like life had pulled so much out of you that you didn't know if you could take one more step? We've all been there, trying to push through in our own strength, only to find it's not enough. Thank God His power isn't dependent on your strength, but activated by your surrender.

When you rely on God, He renews you. His power lifts you above the struggles, the doubts, and the exhaustion. God equips you with what you need to endure. That's the power He promises strength that doesn't fade, no matter how long the journey.

Take your power back and place your hope in the Lord. Shift your focus from what you can't do to what He can. His power is perfected in your weakness and He will carry you through every obstacle. You're not meant to walk this path drained and defeated, you're meant to soar.

Let's Bring It Home:
What's one area of your life where you've been trying to operate in your own strength? Pause, release it to God, and ask Him to fill you with His power. Trust that He will renew your strength in His perfect timing.

Prayer:
Lord, I need Your power today. I'm tired of trying to do things on

my own. Thank You for the promise of renewed strength when I put my hope in You. Help me to trust You fully and to walk in the power You provide. Teach me to soar above my challenges, knowing You are with me every step of the way. In Jesus' name, Amen.

Posture of Compassion

John 13:34-35

"A new command I give you: Love one another. As I have loved you, so you must love one another. By this everyone will know that you are my disciples, if you love one another."

Imagine a mother struggling to juggle her crying baby and her shopping bag rips open on the sidewalk. People just keep walking by. The world doesn't pause for her chaos. Somewhere else, a young woman wipes away silent tears in a crowded room, hoping no one notices her pain because, deep down, she doesn't believe anyone cares enough to ask.

Now imagine someone stopping to gather the woman's spilled groceries, while another holds the baby as she catches her breath. A warm smile and a gentle, "Are you okay?" is offered to the young woman who's trying to hold it together. That's compassion. It doesn't fix everything, but it reminds someone that they're seen, valued, and loved.

Jesus lived this way every day. He didn't just walk by the hurting or brokenhearted; He stopped. He knelt. He, touched. He healed. His love wasn't rushed, calculated, or conditional. It was raw, real, and exactly what the world needed, and still needs today.

Compassion may not always be convenient. But when you choose to love others the way Jesus loved, you make room for God to move through you. You become a reflection of His heart in a way that words alone could never express. Can you demonstrate compassion towards a colleague, or your spouse today?

Let's Bring It Home:

Who in your world could use a touch of compassion today? Look around. Ask God to open your eyes to the need and the courage to step into it. Your small act of love could change someone's entire day—and point them to the love of Christ.

Prayer:

Lord, I want to love like You. Open my eyes to the people around me who need compassion. Soften my heart so I don't just see the need but respond to it. Teach me to love selflessly, even when it's inconvenient. Let my actions be a reflection of Your heart. In Jesus' name, Amen.

Posture of Light

Psalm 119:105

"Your word is a lamp to my feet and a light to my path."

Sometimes, the light you carry will expose what someone's been hiding. It might give them the courage to admit their struggles, to ask for help, or to take a step out of their darkness. God's light has the power to bring healing, clarity, and freedom wherever it shines.

A small act of kindness, a gentle word, or just your presence can be enough to change someone's day, or even their life. The truth is, people are often carrying pain you can't see. They may look fine on the outside, but inside they're battling loneliness, fear, or brokenness. When you allow God's light to shine through you, it's like opening a window in a dark room.

Now, I'm not telling you to neglect your own emotional development. Sometimes being a light will require you to step into uncomfortable places, listen to someone's pain, or stand firm in love when it's easier to look away. Other times, it means simply being present and letting God use you in ways you may never fully understand. The good news is, you don't have to manufacture the light yourself, it comes from staying connected to God's Word and His presence.

God didn't give us His light just for ourselves. He gave it to us so we can carry it into the world, to be a reflection of His love and truth. When you walk in that light, you become part of someone else's testimony. You may never know how your light impacts them, but trust that God is using it to guide them closer to Him.

Let's Bring It Home:
Who might need your light today? Ask God to open your eyes to someone who's struggling and to show you how to reflect His love in their life. Even the smallest gesture could be the light they need to take their next step.

Prayer:
Lord, thank You for the light You've placed in me. Help me to shine it boldly, even in uncomfortable places. Use me to bring healing, hope, and clarity to those who are struggling. Let my life reflect Your love and truth, so others can see You through me. In Jesus' name, Amen.

Posture of Truth

Proverbs 18:21

"The tongue has the power of life and death, and those who love it will eat its fruit."

The truth you carry has power, power to build, power to heal, and yes, even power to destroy. Your words matter, and they carry weight far beyond what you might realize. The Bible reminds us that our tongue holds the power of life and death, and what you choose to speak into the world shapes the lives of others and your own.

Make every effort to align your words with God's Word. It's easy to let emotions or circumstances dictate what we say, but a posture of truth requires intentionality. Choose to speak life when negativity feels more convenient, to uplift instead of tear down, and to share God's truth even when it's uncomfortable.

Sometimes, speaking the truth feels risky. Maybe it's standing firm in your faith when others mock you. Maybe it's gently confronting a loved one with love and grace because you care about their well-being. But when you posture yourself in truth, your words become a reflection of God's heart. They have the power to cut through lies, eradicate confusion, and shine light in darkness.

A life rooted in truth becomes a testimony that draws others closer to Christ.

Let's Bring It Home:
Think about the words you've been speaking lately—to yourself, to others, and even in prayer. Are they rooted in truth and life? Ask

God to guide your words and to help you align your speech with
His truth, knowing the power they carry.

Prayer:
Lord, thank You for the truth of Your Word and the power it holds.
Help me to use my words to speak life, to build others up, and to
reflect Your love. Teach me to live in truth, not just in what I say
but in how I act. Let everything I speak and do bring honor to You.
In Jesus' name, Amen.

Posture of Worship

Psalm 100:2-4

"Worship the Lord with gladness; come before Him with joyful songs. Know that the Lord is God. It is He who made us, and we are His; we are His people, the sheep of His pasture. Enter His gates with thanksgiving and His courts with praise; give thanks to Him and praise His name."

Worship is so much more than a song or a Sunday morning activity. It's a way of living that declares, "God, You are worthy." It's waking up with gratitude, choosing to praise Him in the middle of a storm, and bowing your heart in surrender to His will. Worship flows from a place of knowing who God is. The Creator who made you, the Shepherd who leads you, and the Savior who loves you unconditionally.

Think about this, every time you worship, you step into God's presence. Worship connects you to God's heart, aligning your perspective with His and reminding you of His greatness. But worship is also about what you bring to God. It's entering His gates with thanksgiving, not just for what He's done but for who He is. It's lifting up your voice, not because everything is perfect, but because He is faithful. Worship shifts the atmosphere, it shifts your heart. It takes your focus off of your problems and places it on His power and goodness.

True worship happens when you stop looking at your circumstances and start looking at God. Declaring, "God, You are bigger than anything I face, and I trust You with it all."

Let's Bring It Home:
When was the last time you worshiped God, not for what He's done, but simply because of who He is? Take a moment today to

intentionally worship Him—through a song, a prayer, or even a quiet moment of reflection. Let gratitude lead you into His presence.

Prayer:
Lord, I worship You because You are good, faithful, and worthy of all my praise. Thank You for creating me, loving me, and never leaving me. Help me to live a life of worship, where my heart, words, and actions reflect Your glory. Let my praise bring me closer to You, no matter what season I'm in. In Jesus' name, Amen.

Posture of Boldness

Matthew 17:20

"He replied, 'Because you have so little faith. Truly I tell you, if you have faith as small as a mustard seed, you can say to this mountain, 'Move from here to there,' and it will move. Nothing will be impossible for you.'"

Posturing yourself in boldness does not always mean you will be the loudest and most fearless. But instead having the courage to step out on faith, even when fear is whispering in your ear. It's looking at the mountain in front of you also known as "the problem" and choosing to believe that God's power is bigger than anything standing in your way.

Jesus didn't say you needed huge, perfect faith to move mountains. He said all you need is faith the size of a mustard seed small but planted. That's the key. Boldness grows when you take small steps of faith and act on it. Maybe it's praying for something you've been too scared to ask for. Maybe it's standing firm in a decision God told you to make. Or maybe it's speaking life into a situation everyone else has given up on.

When you posture yourself in boldness, you're declaring, "God, I believe You're able." It's stepping out of the boat like Peter, knowing the waves are high but keeping your eyes on Jesus. It's saying to the mountain, "Move," even when it looks like it hasn't budged yet. Boldness trusts that God is already working, even when you can't see it.

Boldness is contagious, too. When others see you standing in faith, speaking life, and walking in God's promises, it inspires them to do the same. Your boldness can be the spark someone else needs to trust God with their own mountains.

Let's Bring It Home:
What mountain are you facing right now? What step of boldness is God asking you to take? Take that small seed of faith, plant it in action, and trust God to move on your behalf.

Prayer:
Lord, help me to walk in boldness today. Even when fear tries to creep in, remind me that You are greater than any obstacle I face. Teach me to trust Your promises and to take steps of faith, no matter how small they feel. Let my boldness point others to Your power and glory. In Jesus' name, Amen.

Posture of Transformation

2 Corinthians 5:17

"Therefore, if anyone is in Christ, the new creation has come: The old has gone, the new is here!"

Some people think transformation is merely just getting a new leash on life; But it's more than that it's the act of becoming someone completely new. When you step into Christ, you're not just turning over a new leaf, you're stepping into a whole new life. The old version of you, the mistakes, the shame, the baggage is gone! God doesn't patch you up; He transforms you completely from the inside out, making you into a new creation.

Transformation starts in your heart and flows into every part of your life. It's a process, not an overnight event. When you posture yourself for transformation, you're surrendering to God's work in you. You're saying, "Lord, take my life and make it Yours." It means letting go of who you used to be and embracing who God is shaping you to become.

Release things you've held onto for far too long: old habits, toxic relationships, or mindsets that no longer serve who God is calling you to be. The beauty of transformation is ongoing. Every day, as you walk with Christ, He continues to shape and mold you. He renews your mind, strengthens your spirit, and helps you reflect His love more and more. And as you're transformed, your life becomes a testimony. Others will see the change in you and be drawn to the One who made it possible.

Let's Bring It Home:
What's one area of your life where you feel God is calling you to change or grow? Ask Him to help you release the old and embrace

the new. Trust that He is working for you, even if you can't see the full picture yet.

Prayer:
Lord, thank You for making me new in You. Help me to let go of the old and fully step into the life You've called me to live. Transform my heart, mind, and actions so that I reflect Your love and grace. Use my life as a testimony of Your power and goodness. In Jesus' name, Amen.

Posture of Seeking

Matthew 6:33

"But seek first His kingdom and His righteousness, and all these things will be given to you as well."

Seeking God is a way of life. It's waking up each day with a heart tuned to His voice, a mind focused on His truth, and a soul longing for His presence. When you posture yourself to seek Him first, your posture says, "Lord, You're my priority. Your will, Your way, and Your kingdom come before anything else."

The demands of life, the noise of social media, and the pull of our own desires can make it hard to focus. That's why seeking requires intentionality. It's about carving out time in your day to pray, to read His Word, and to listen for His guidance. It's choosing Him over comfort, convenience, or quick fixes.

The beauty of seeking God is that it always leads to finding Him. He's not hiding. He's waiting for you to draw near so He can meet you with His peace, wisdom, and direction. When you seek Him first, everything else falls into place because your heart aligns with His purpose.

Seeking also builds trust. The more you seek Him, the more you'll see His hand at work in your life.

Let's Bring It Home:
What does seeking God look like in your life right now? Is there a space where you need to intentionally invite Him in—your decisions, your time, or your relationships? Take a moment today to pause, pray, and seek Him first.

Prayer:
Lord, I want to seek You with my whole heart. Help me to quiet the distractions around me and to focus on You. Teach me to trust Your plans and to pursue Your will above my own. Thank You for the promise that when I seek You, I will find You. In Jesus' name, Amen.

Posture of Promise

2 Peter 1:3-4

"His divine power has given us everything we need for a godly life through our knowledge of Him who called us by His own glory and goodness. Through these He has given us His very great and precious promises, so that through them you may participate in the divine nature, having escaped the corruption in the world caused by evil desires."

Every posture we've explored from trust, to faithfulness, courage, prayer, and beyond has led us here, to the promise. The promise that God has already equipped you with everything you need to live the life He's called you to. The promise that His power, His presence, and His purpose are more than enough for whatever you face.

Think about it. When you trust Him, you find peace. When you stand in faith, mountains move. When you pray, you connect with His heart. When you seek Him, you find purpose. And when you live in boldness, love, and compassion, you show the world who He is. A God who never fails.

As you close this book, remember this: His promises are certain, His power is limitless, and His presence is constant. Every time you adjust your posture to reflect Him, you are participating in a mission greater than yourself.

Now it's time to walk in His promises. Take the trust you've built, the faith you've cultivated, the courage you've claimed, and the love you've shared, and live boldly for Him. Let every posture you take point back to His glory.

Let's Bring It Home:
You've been given everything you need. How will you live out His

promises today? Take a moment to reflect on the postures you've learned and ask God to help you carry them into your daily life, trusting in His faithfulness every step of the way.

Final Prayer:
Lord, thank You for the promises You've spoken over my life. Thank You for equipping me with everything I need to walk in Your purpose. As I go forward, help me to trust You completely, seek You faithfully, and reflect Your love boldly. Let every posture of my heart, mind, and spirit honor You and draw others closer to You. May my life be a testimony of Your power, grace, and glory. In Jesus' name, Amen.

A Final Word

This ain't goodbye. Your journey doesn't end here. Share your testimony of how these postures have transformed your life. Visit rainbowcoach.org and share your story, leave a review, or join a small group discussion. Together, we can inspire others to align their hearts with God's purpose. I know we've covered a lot in these pages, and maybe some of it stirred up things you weren't ready to face or reminded you of the areas where God has been tugging at your heart. But let me tell you this: You've got what it takes because you've got Him.

Every posture we've talked about isn't just for "those people" who seem to have it all together. It's for *you*. The you that's been through hell and high water, the you that's tired of trying to figure it all out on your own, the you that's still standing even after life knocked you down. God has been with you the whole time, and He's not going anywhere.

I need you to hear this: God sees you. He loves you on your best days and your worst days. His promises don't change just because you've made mistakes or feel unworthy. Every time you choose to posture yourself before Him—whether it's in trust, surrender, or worship—He shows up. Every single time.

So now, as you close this book, the real work begins. Take these postures into your everyday life. Carry them into the moments when you feel strong and the moments when you feel weak. Remember that you don't have to be perfect; you just have to be willing. Let God handle the rest.

I'm praying for you. I'm rooting for you. And I believe with everything in me that the best is still ahead. Keep pressing, keep praying, and keep posturing yourself before the One who holds it all together.

You've got this, because He's got you.

With all my love and prayers,
Valencia "Coach V" Gibson

"He who began a good work in you will carry it on to completion until the day of Christ Jesus."
– Philippians 1:6

Stay connected with me! I'd love to hear how God is moving in your life and how this devotional has blessed you. Reach out at *rainbowcoach.org* or find me on **IG: @therealrainbowcoach**. Let's keep walking this journey together!

Appendix: Summary of Postures

Posture	Key Scripture	Core Idea	Practical Action
Posture of Trust	Proverbs 3:5-6	Trusting God frees us from fear and anxiety, helping us rest in His promises.	Release control and surrender areas of fear to God in prayer.
Posture of Faith	2 Corinthians 5:7	Faith means stepping forward even when the path isn't clear.	Take small, intentional steps of faith, trusting God with the results.
Posture of Prayer	Philippians 4:6-7	Prayer exchanges worry for peace and connects us to God's heart.	Make space daily for heartfelt, honest communication with G
Posture of Courage	Isaiah 41:10	Courage is walking in God's strength instead of fear.	Name your fears and declare God's promise of presence and help over them.
Posture of Love	Romans 8:38-39	God's love is steady and unshakable, enabling us to love others selflessly.	Reflect on God's love for you, a extend that love to someone difficult to love.
Posture of Rest	Matthew 11:28-30	Rest is an act of faith that trusts God with our burdens.	Pause your busyness to connec with God and let Him renew yo strength.

sture of ength	2 Corinthians 12:9-10	God's strength is perfected in our weakness.	Identify an area of weakness and invite God to show His power through it.
sture of Joy	James 1:2-4	Joy comes from knowing that trials produce growth and perseverance.	Find one way to praise God amidst a challenge you are facing.
sture of rrender	Matthew 16:24-25	Surrender is not defeat but giving over control to God.	Write down what you need to release and pray for the courage to let God take over.
sture of Grace	Ephesians 2:8-9	God's grace is undeserved, unearned, and freely given.	Let go of guilt and rest in the gift of grace by journaling ways you've seen it in your life.
sture of rgiveness	Matthew 6:14-15	Forgiveness is a choice to release bitterness and reflect God's grace.	Write a letter (even if unsent) to someone you need to forgive or ask forgiveness from.
sture of rpose	Jeremiah 29:11	God has a specific and hopeful purpose for your life.	Reflect on a current struggle and ask God to reveal how He is working through it.
sture of ithfulness	Lamentations 3:22-23	Faith is found in the small gestures like being consistent, trusting and obeying God daily.	Think about how God has been faithful in your life. Write down one way He's shown His love and compassion recently.

Posture of Protection	Proverbs 4:23	Protect your heart with God's Word and His promises, you're building a strong foundation that nothing can shake.	Take a moment to reflect on what's influencing your heart right now. Is it bringing you closer to God or pulling you away?
Posture of Wisdom	James 1:5	Wisdom causes you to trust God to lead you step by step, even when the full picture isn't clear.	Think about a decision or challenge you're facing right now. Have you asked God for wisdom about it?
Posture of Peace	Posture of Peace	Posturing yourself for peace means choosing trust over fear, faith over anxiety, and surrender over managing every detail of life.	What's been weighing on your heart lately? Imagine handing each one over to God
Posture of Fruitfulness	Galatians 5:22-23	When the Spirit of God is at work in you, His fruit begins to show.	Spend time today inviting God to nurture that fruit and to help you reflect His goodness in practical everyday ways.
Posture of Renewal	Romans 12:2	Renewal is a process of transformation that starts in your mind.	Spend a few moments reflecting on how His Word can reshape your thinking and lead you into transformation.
Posture of Calm	Philippians 4:7	Calm is a posture that comes from knowing God's peace is greater than any circumstance you face..	Invite God's peace to guard your heart and mind. Remind yourself that His presence is greater than your circumstances.

sture of edience	John 14:15	Obedience is a reflection of our love for God, choosing His will over our desires.	Identify one area where you feel God calling you to obey and take a step toward it today.
sture of tience	Ecclesiastes 3:1	Patience teaches us to rely on Him, to strengthen our faith, and to recognize His blessings when they come.	How does that memory encourage you in what you're waiting for now?
sture of wer	Isaiah 40:29-31	His power is perfected in your weakness and He will carry you through every obstacle.	Pause, release it to God, and ask Him to fill you with His power.
sture of mpassion	John 13:34-35	Compassion doesn't fix everything, but it reminds someone that they're seen, valued, and loved.	Ask God to open your eyes to the need and the courage to step into it.
sture of Light	Psalm 119:105	God's light has the power to bring healing, clarity, and freedom wherever it shines.	Even the smallest gesture could be the light they need to take their next step.
sture of Truth	Proverbs 18:21	The truth you carry has power, power to build, power to heal, and yes, even power to destroy.	Think about the words you've been speaking lately—to yourself, to others, and even in prayer.
sture of orship	Psalm 100:2-4	Worship connects you to God's heart.	Take a moment today to intentionally worship Him through a song, a prayer, or even a quiet moment of reflection.

Posture of Boldness	Matthew 17:20	When you posture yourself in boldness, you're declaring, "God, I believe You're able."	What step of boldness is God asking you to take?
Posture of Transformation	2 Corinthians 5:17	Transformation starts in your heart and flows into every part of your life.	Ask God to help you release the old and embrace the new.
Posture of Seeking	Matthew 6:33	The beauty of seeking God is that it always leads to finding Him. He's not hiding.	Is there a space where you need to intentionally invite Him in your decisions, your time, or your relationships?
Posture of Promise	2 Peter 1:3-4	His promises are certain, His power is limitless, and His presence is constant.	You've been given everything you need. How will you live out His promises today?

WHAT ARE YOU DECLARING?

www.ingramcontent.com/pod-product-compliance
Lightning Source LLC
Chambersburg PA
CBHW050740150726
48196CB00003B/289